Contents

What are air sports?

Welcome to the thrilling world of air sports. This is a world where competitors **soar** above the earth and where people actually fly!

4

AIR
SPORTS

Ellen Labrecque

www.raintreepublishers.co.uk
Visit our website to find out more information about Raintree books.

To order:

☎ Phone 0845 6044371

🖹 Fax +44 (0) 1865 312263

🖳 Email myorders@raintreepublishers.co.uk

Customers from outside the UK please telephone +44 1865 312262

Raintree is an imprint of Capstone Global Library Limited, a company incorporated in England and Wales having its registered office at 7 Pilgrim Street, London, EC4V 6LB – Registered company number: 6695582

Edited by Rebecca Rissman, Dan Nunn, and Catherine Veitch
Designed by Joanna Hinton Malivoire
Picture research by Ruth Blair
Originated by Capstone Global Library
Printed and bound in China by CTPS

ISBN 978 1 406 22690 4 (harback)
15 14 13 12 11
10 9 8 7 6 5 4 3 2 1

ISBN 978 1 406 22697 3 (paperback)
16 15 14 13 12
10 9 8 7 6 5 4 3 2 1

British Library Cataloguing in Publication Data
Labrecque, Ellen
Air sports. – (Extreme sport)
797.5-dc22
A full catalogue record for this book is available from the British Library.

Acknowledgements
We would like to thank the following for permission to reproduce photographs: Alamy pp. 15 (© Alun Richardson), 22 (© David Sims); Corbis pp. 5 (© Ken Glaser), 6 (© Benelux), 7 (© Bettmann), 9 (© Alain Revel, Rene Robert, Jean-Luc Boivin/Sygma), 10 (© HO/Reuters), 12 (© Jim Sugar), 13 (© Kevin Fleming), 21 (© Mark Newman—Rainbow/Science Faction), 24 (© Photo Japan/Robert Harding World Imagery), 25 (© Alessandro Bianchi/Reuters), 26 (© Sam Diephuis); Getty Images pp. 8 (Bob Bird), 11 (Helmut Tucek), 19 (Dean Mouhtaropoulos); Shutterstock pp. 4 (© Germanskydiver), 14 (© Aleksandar Todorovic), 16 (© Graham Prentice), 17 (© Mihai Dancaescu), 18 (© homydesign), 20 (© JanJar), 23 (© Oleksii Abramov), 27 (© Germanskydiver), 28 (© G Tipene), 29 (© Monkey Business Images).

Cover photograph of skydivers jumping from an aeroplane reproduced with permission of Corbis (© Moodboard).

Every effort has been made to contact copyright holders of material reproduced in this book. Any omissions will be rectified in subsequent printings if notice is given to the publisher.

Some words are shown in bold, **like this**. You can find out what they mean by looking in the glossary.

STAY SAFE!
Remember, though, many of these sports should be left to the **experts**!

Skydiving

Want to touch the clouds? Then give skydiving a try. Skydiving is when a person jumps from a moving aircraft. After **free falling** through the air, the jumper opens a parachute and comes to a soft landing.

WOW!

Joseph Kittinger holds the record for the highest, fastest, and longest skydive. In 1960, he jumped from an aircraft and reached speeds of 988 kilometres an hour!

BASE jumping

BASE jumping is like skydiving, but more dangerous. A jumper leaps from a fixed object such as a building, a bridge, or a cliff. The jumper has just seconds to open his or her parachute.

Wingsuit flying

Want to fly through the air like a superhero? In wingsuit flying, athletes put on a special wingsuit made from **fabric**. The suit helps lift up the body. A flight ends with a parachute opening, so the flyer can land safely.

WOW!

In 2003, Austrian daredevil Felix Baumgartner flew across the English Channel in a wingsuit. He travelled at 360 kilometres an hour. That's the same speed as a racing car!

Hang-gliding

A hang-gliding pilot flies an aircraft without a motor. The pilot is **suspended** in a **harness** below the hang glider. The pilot takes off by pushing off the ground with his feet. He steers the aircraft by moving his body.

WOW!
Hang-gliders can **soar** hundreds of kilometres for hours at a time! The longest flight on record is over 11 hours!

Paragliding

Paragliding and hang-gliding are similar. Both have a pilot who sits in a **harness** underneath a **fabric** wing. However, a paraglider is like a parachute, whereas a hang-glider has a metal frame.

WOW!

The furthest a paraglider has ever flown is 504 kilometres. That is about half the length of Britain.

Gliding

Imagine flying your own plane ... without an engine! To get **soaring** the glider is pulled with a **tow rope** by a powered aircraft. Once released, the glider can soar for hundreds of kilometres.

glider

WOW!

Gliding competitions are held all over the world. There are racing and **aerobatic** competitions. Aerobatic competitions are where the gliders perform tricks.

Air racing

Get your eyes on the sky! Air racing involves small aircraft racing one another through air gates. The aircraft only fly about 20 metres in the air, so fans can watch closely. The pilots are fast and skilled. If they miss the gates, they are **penalized**.

air gate

18

WOW!
In New York City in June 2010, pilots raced around the Statue of Liberty!

Hot air ballooning

People have been flying in hot air balloons for over 200 years. Hot air balloons are powered by hot air shot through a burner. The hot air helps the balloon rise through the cooler air.

WOW!
In 1999, two men flew a hot air balloon around the world. It took them just under 20 days to complete the trip.

Kitesurfing

Kitesurfing is also called kiteboarding. A kitesurfer hooks his or her feet on to a small surfboard. Then, she uses a kite and the wind to pull herself through the water!

WOW!

Kirsty Jones of Wales holds the kitesurfing distance world record. She travelled from an island near Spain to Morocco in Africa. The trip took over 9 hours!

23

Kite fighting

Kite fighting is serious business in many Asian countries. The object of a fight is to cut the other person's string and knock the kite down. Kite fighting can be one-on-one, or between a lot of people. The kite left flying is the winner.

WOW!

Fighter kites are made with strings of munja. Munja is a type of grass that is as sharp as a razor blade.

Be safe!

Air sports can be exciting, wild, and thrilling. But they can also be dangerous and scary.

Do not try any of these sports on your own. Listen to **experts** and have many lessons before trying these sports. You must always make sure you wear all the proper **equipment** needed for a safe ride.

Get fit!

Having strong arms is important for many sports. The stronger arms and shoulders you have, the better athlete you will be. Try this arm exercise.

From a standing position, extend your arms straight out from your body. **Rotate** your arms in a forward motion making small circles. Gradually increase the size of the circles until you are making big circles. Do this for 2–4 minutes at a time.

Glossary

aerobatic stunts performed in flight

equipment tools or clothing that you need

expert person with a special skill or knowledge

fabric cloth made by weaving or knitting

free falling fall from something very quickly, from a great height

harness safety equipment and straps used to support someone

penalized punished or put at a disadvantage. For example, by being given a time penalty when extra time is added to the race time of a sportsperson.

rotate turn around a central point

soar fly or rise up high into the air

suspended hang by attachment to something

tow rope strong line used to pull something along

Find out more

Books

Hang Gliding and Paragliding, Noel Whittall (TickTock, 2009)

Project X: Adrenalin Rush, Alex Lane (OUP, 2009)

Skydiving, Lesley Gale (TickTock, 2009)

Xtreme Sports: Base Jumping, Sue L. Hamilton (Abdo Publishing, 2010)

Websites

http://www.bbc.co.uk/northernireland/schools/4_11/uptoyou/
This website has lots of information about healthy eating and exercise. Why not get fit and enjoy those extreme sports?

http://kidshealth.org/kid/stay_healthy/food/sports.html
Find out more about eating well and playing sports.

http://readyforten.com/skills/81-kite-flying
Learn some tips and tricks for flying a kite.

Index